BLOGOSPHERES

SUBASH M R

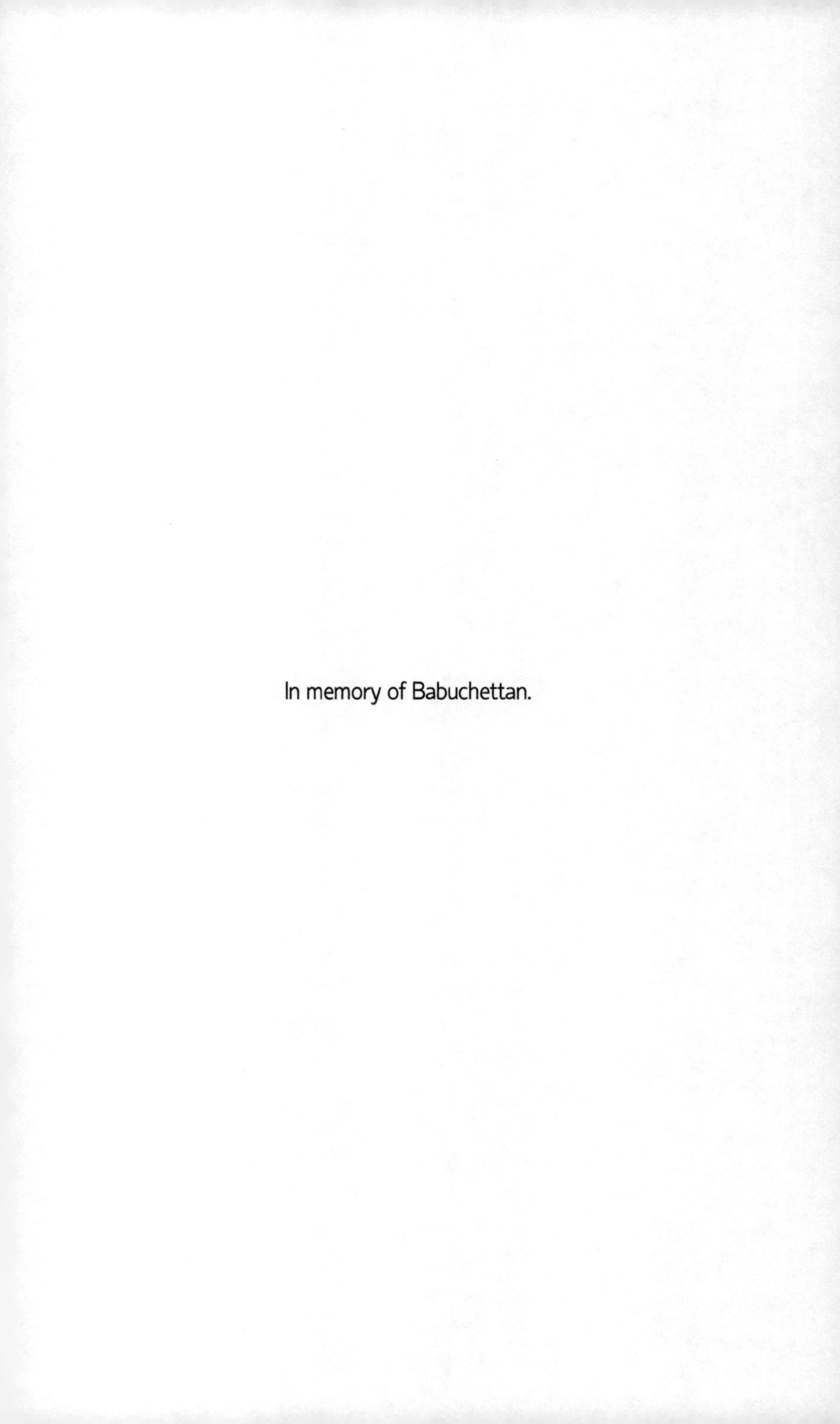

In memory of Babuchettan.

Contents

Foreword

Blogospheres go from A to B alphabetically from one topic to another from actor Amitabh Bachchan to His Highness Ayyappa Swamy in this book from beginning to end chronologically.

It is very interesting to read to see how the writer is juggling several topics simultaneously in the air by skillful way of narration and wits, which will certainly be appreciated by the Joe Bloggs and Joe Blow and much less than the Joe Public.

CHAPTER ONE

AGEISM

When one becomes older, he needs to be treated fairly? Doesn't he! It is universally true that in whichever field, when people are getting old, chances and opportunities fade. For example, in the field of sports, cinema and politics, etc. For that, legal profession is one of the exceptions, wherein, value of a lawyer will increase as he or she becomes old.

Stop singing when voice is good is the policy to escape from those situations wherein prejudices and discrimination were governed on the ground of a person's age. In politics, an exception is Fidel Alejandro Castro Ruz who governed the republic of Cuba as Prime Minister from 1959 to 1976 and then as President from 1976 to 2008. Fidel Castro is the longest-ruling non-royal national leader since 1900 by term length 52 years and 62 days.

Ram Boolchand Jethmalani is a senior lawyer who announced his retirement at the age of 94 from judicial profession spreading over seven-decade –long career on 10th September 2017. He was speaking at a function organized by apex bar body, the Bar Council of India, to felicitate new Chief Justice of India Justice Dipak Misra.

"I am here just to tell you I am retiring from the profession but I am taking on a new role as long as I am alive."

Mr.Ram Jethmalani was one of the highest-paid lawyers in the country at the time of his voluntary retirement on his field. How many are there to announce their voluntary retirement on their respective fields to give way to new generation to come. Very difficult to find out any, but those who are on the go now let them go on but remind them one thing that never ever shall have the occasion to go through the disappointment on the aged prejudices, but certainly one can avoid it if he or she takes appropriate actions at appropriate times.

The irony is that in some fields age is considered as experience but in some other fields it is considered as disqualification. In academic field, age is always related to learning and experience of wisdom, on the other hand, in cinema field, age is a curse for most of the film stars who have fallen off from their stardom due to the discrimination on the basis of their old age. In our times, Amitabh Bachchan is one of the living exceptions. At the age of 79, he is going stronger and stronger without being affected by age related adversities or discrimination in his own field. Of all, health is wealth.

Not only in the field of sports, but in some other fields also such as Army, Navy including Air Force and as well other jobs for example air hostess job, age is considered as one of the determining factors in respect of the each and every specific job mentioned above. Teaching and medical practice are also exempted from this age bar clause. Little Master Sachin Ramesh Tendulkar had to announce his retirement from ODIs in December 2012. He retired from Twenty 20 cricket in October 2013 and subsequently retired from all forms of cricket on 16 November 2013 after playing his 200th Test match, against the West Indies in Mumbai's Wankhede Stadium at the age of 39 even though there is no age limit proscribed especially in cricket and in sports generally.

Ageing is a natural phenomenon and disappointment and despair should not be its by-products. We can make it healthier than before if we realize where we have reached. It is not an ending point, but a beginning one. It should be like every rupee is earned is hard earned as every year is lived is hard lived. Let nobody cut a sorry figure in his or her old age.

Sachin Tendulkar, Amitabh Bachchan, Ram Jethmalani and Fidel Castro are exceptional personalities who have set up their own footprint in their respective fields to be followed by the coming generations. Age is just a number which changes after year and year, but what matters is health, the state of being free from illness or injury, a person's mental or physical condition, on this ground, only on this medical ground only, a person may be replaced or allowed to retire from his or her area of working. So, criterion should not be age, but health.

This is era of electronic media. This is in contrast to static media (mainly print media) Broadcast or storage media that take advantage of electronic technology. The term "electronic media" is often used in contrast with print media. Print media, i.e., newspapers, magazines have a short life, as people normally get rid of them after one reading. While digital media offers rapid, real–time engagement opportunities with its viewers. The debaters are changed frequently according to the debating topic.

Is professional journalism dying due to the technological advancements occurred in digital journalism is under debate. Are writing and reporting in traditional journalism becoming irrelevant due to the electronic advancement happened in digital media, such as TV and Blog, etc.?!

It seems that traditional journalism has been replaced by digital journalism which has again reduced to debate journalism in digital media. In the name of interactive journalism, debaters will beat about the bush on a particular issue over a period of time, minimum I hour. Some editors are promoters for specific political positions. They will do *Hanuman Seva* while mediating the debate is usual. It is not at all beat reporting on a particular issue over a period of chunk time.

Days of a year are like strands of hair on a person's head which fall around the whole year and finally an old year is out and a new year is in. Wish a happy new year to each and every person who is reading this.

CHAPTER TWO

HAPPINESS!?

Wealth cannot buy full happiness which shall be attained by aestheticism only. Measuring happiness in terms of wealth is an old-fashioned method and moreover happiness is not synonymous with wealth at all. Does one get full-fledged happiness with one's wealth? Nope. Money is not everything and it cannot alone bring happiness to one's life!

The world revolves around imaginations and realities become sometimes fallacies! Five feet and six inch above is over height and five feet below is under height, similarly, above seventy is considered as overweight and below fifty is considered as underweight to a person is concerned.

When a person is walking on foot in this earth, where cats, dogs, and even tigers and lions are walking about. So, comparing a person to these creatures, a person's height and weight shall not be above and below and over and under as mentioned herein above for aesthetic reasons.

It is always boring to having above and below and over and under height and weight. It does not mean unattractive. Nonetheless of one's height, weight and even color and gender, attraction happens, a person may be attractive even though he or she may be above or below height or over or under weight or black or white in complexion. Attractiveness has nothing to do with one's height, weight, gender and even color nevertheless?!

In a nutshell, creature comforts and well-being are the basics of happiness. These are universal basic human needs and that happiness results from its fulfilment. Happiness may be added up to one's day to day living by enjoyment, entertainment, learning, satisfaction and experience, etc.

Watching debates on television is one of the means to get educated and at the same time get amused. Television debate has a history of about six decades and on September 26, 1960, presidential candidates Richard M.Nixon and John F.Kennedy stood before cameras for the first-ever televised presidential debate.

Over the period of time, debates have become one of the main items of broadcast on T V across the world, thereby its' worth has been compromised and undervalued like present time presidents and political leaders.

We get information and knowledge out of televisions debates to a certain extent, but at the same time get fun and amusement while watching debates on television, wherein experts on various topics or spin doctors of several political parties are participated on daily basis for discussion and analysis on the given talking point.

Suppose, some news anchors while conducting debates on their televisions on any matter under the sun, pass questions from a debater to another one abruptly when the former is talking, without knowing this the first one was talking out of on screen and seeing this is an instant joke all the time whenever it happens on screen, and the sorry state of affair is that the talking heads do not even show the courtesy to say the debaters that they would come back to them while passing questions from one to another! The fun factor of all these tea shop debates are those instances of the said cross-talk.

And also, statements issuing by some community leaders from time to time pertaining to any sensational court rulings or on the general matters are laughable while seeing it on televisions or reading it in the newspapers. The square leaders who are laughing stocks as well as happy hunting ground! Besides, seeing and hearing justification of chief ministers for every wrong doings of their party cadre and above all government's machinery and as well as prime ministers for their phonetics are all matters of interest and importance. Cultivating personal strengths and resources, like humor, social/animal company, and daily occupations, also appears to help people preserve acceptable levels of SWB despite the presence of symptoms of depression, anxiety, and stress.

Wealth is not fail-safe in case of relationships, especially in troubled marriages! Money does not make a go of even a short term or a long-term marriage whatsoever! It is applicable for the planet's richest person or the poorest person. The word 'Failure' is antonym to happiness! Whether the all the failed marriages are due to the lack of income or wealth? Good mental health and good relationship contribute more than income to happiness. It is not necessary that all rich persons must be happy and at the same time, all the poor persons must be unhappy.

In the *Nicomachean Ethics*, written in 350 BCE, Aristotle stated that happiness (also being well and doing well) is the only thing that humans desire for its own sake, unlike riches, honor, health or friendship. Thus understood, the happy life is the good life, that is, a life in which a person fulfils human nature in an excellent way. Thus, according to Aristotle, the life of excellent rational activity is the happy life. This second-best life is the life of moral virtue.

Quotient of Happiness

Happiness's definition and philosophy varies from religion to religion and its psychology and theories are the subject of debate on usage and meaning and on possible differences in understanding by culture. Measurement of happiness depends upon relationships to physical characteristics, possible limits of happiness seeking and economical and political views.

Happiness is used in the context of mental or emotional states, including positive or pleasant emotions ranging from contentment to intense joy. It is also used in the context of life satisfaction, subjective well-being, eudaimonia, flourishing and well-being.

Well-Being

Well-being or wellness is the condition of an individual or group. A high level of well-being means that in some sense the individual's or group's condition is positive. According to Corey Keyes, mental well-being has three components, namely emotional or subjective well-being, psychological well-being, and social well-being. Keys model of mental well-being has received extensive empirical support across cultures.

Positive Psychology

Well-being is a central concept in positive psychology. Positive psychology is concerned with eudaimonia, "the good life", reflection about what holds the greatest value in life-The factors that contribute the most to a well-lived and fulfilling life. While not attempting a strict definition of the good life, positive psychologists agree that one must live a happy, engaged, and meaningful life in order to experience "the good life". Martin Seligman referred to "the good life" as using your signature strengths every day to produce authentic happiness and abundant gratification.

Subjective Well-Being

Subjective well-being encompasses moods and emotions as well as evaluations of one's satisfaction with general and specific areas of one's life. Concepts encompassed by subjective well-being include happiness.

Subjective well-being tends to stable over time and is strongly related to personal traits. There is evidence that health and SWB may mutually influence each other, as good health tends to be associated with great happiness, and a number of studies have found that positive emotions and optimism can have beneficial influence on health.

Quality of life has also been studied as conceptualization of SWB. Although its exact definition varies, it is usually measured as an aggregation of well-being across several life domains and may include both subjective and objective components.

On moderation and in average happiness rests to say height, weight, wealth, creed, greed including sex and procreation of children are all about happiness, but in terms of its degree in average and on moderation only.

Since the 1960, happiness research has been conducted in a wide variety of scientific disciplines, including gerontology, social psychology, clinical and medical research and happiness economics. The implied meaning of the word may vary depending on context, qualifying happiness as a polysemous and a fuzzy concept. Some users accept these issues, but continue to use the word because of its convening power. According to Sonja Lyubomirsky, the determinants of happiness are a combination of a person's genetic set-point, intentional activities and life circumstances. But the real beatitudes may be feeling seeing and knowing the stone, thorn, trees, animals, planet and space, etc. except human beings?!

CHAPTER THREE

HOW HOLY IS HOLLYWOOD?

Hollywood is a neighborhood in the central region of Los Angeles, California. This densely populated neighborhood is notable as the home of the U.S. Film Industry, including several of its historic studios, and its name has come to be a shorthand reference for the industry and the people associated with it.

Hollywood was a small community in 1870 and was incorporated as Municipality in 1903.It was consolidated with the city of Los Angeles in 1910, and soon thereafter a prominent film industry emerged, eventually becoming the most recognized film industry in the World.

Los Angeles became the capital of the film industry. The mountains, plains and low land prices made Hollywood a good place to establish film studios.

Hollywood became known as Tinsel town and the dream factory because of the glittering image of the movie industry. Hollywood has since a major Centre for film study in the United States.

Hollywood has become synonymous with sexual assault and sexual abuse in the recent times due to the "#Me Too" campaign, which stirred in by October 31, 2017 on social media! Why? It is a million or billions dollar question that everybody wants to ask. Here, if the term assault or abuse does not begin with prefix 'sexual', then it means mere assault or abuse. Not otherwise. Assault or abuse are as old as humankind or time immemorial. But what about sexual assault or sexual abuse. Who was the first victim of it? Man or woman? Its answer would be like what came first the chicken or the egg.

Assault is defined that whoever makes any gesture, or any preparation intending or knowing it to be likely that such gesture or preparation will cause any person present to apprehend that he or she who makes that gesture or preparation is about to use criminal force to that person, is said to commit assault.

Mere words do not amount to an assault. But the words which a person uses may give to his gestures or preparation such a meaning as may make those gestures or preparations amount to an assault.

Under the definition of the sexual harassment, demand or request for sexual favors also comes. It is against the gender equality. Is it possible to prevent sexual harassment in the showbiz through judicial process? Gender equality includes protection from sexual harassment and right to work with dignity, which is a universally recognized basic human right.

Hollywood or Bollywood or any other wood or woods, are there the law of the jungle prevailing or rule of law. The flicks industry where relationships are as fragile as glasses and for certain groups, especially women and disadvantaged people, it is still a glass ceiling.

Marriages are made in heaven, but broken down easily like bubbles in motion picture industry! Tournament behavior in which relations tends to be highly polygamous because high levels of male-male and female-female ambition and competition.

The fundamental right to carry on any occupation, trade or profession depends on the availability of a safe working environment. Right to life means life with dignity. Instances of continuous sexual harassment in this field resulting in violation of fundamental rights of artists are brought before the general public in the recent past. To provide for the effective enforcement of the basic human right of gender equality and guarantee against sexual harassment and abuse, more particularly against sexual harassment at workplaces, especially in show business, guidelines and norms are to be laid down for strict observance at all workplaces. The common minimum requirement of this right has received global acceptance.

In view of the prevailing scenario in which the violation of these rights is not uncommon. With the increasing awareness and emphasis on gender justice, there is increase in the efforts to guard against such violations and the resentment towards incidents of sexual harassment is also increasing. The perpetrator who may either be a male or a female, but he or she can't be compared to an animal or his or her behavior can't be compared to that of animalism. A perpetrator of sexual harassment may at least, be compared to such other sexual perpetrator.

Equality in employment can be seriously impaired when actors are subjected to gender violence, such as sexual harassment in the workplace. Where any of these acts is committed in circumstances where under the victim of such conduct has a reasonable apprehension that in relation to the victim's job or work whether he or she is drawing salary, or honorarium or voluntary, such conduct can be humiliating and may constitute a health and safety problem.

There is no reason why the international conventions and norms cannot, therefore, be used for construing the fundamental rights expressly guaranteed which embody the basic concept of gender equality in all spheres of human activity that prohibits of discrimination on grounds of religion, race, caste, sex or place of birth.

Discrimination on the ground of race, sex or age, etc. are all human rights violations in terms of a victim's fundamental rights are concerned and the casting couch mentality, wages disparity and nepotism leading the way for (crestfallen) awards are all pointing to the good, the bad and the ugly sides of the film industry. There is always more to a story that meets the eye.

In this limelight business, everything is possible under the sun. It is an emotional industry after all. Most actors are low in education but high on emotion. These lowbrow classes of people are earning Millions or Billions at the cost of viewers' sentiments.

In Indywood too things are not different. In Bollywood, the term being a portmanteau of "Bombay" (now Mumbai) and "Hollywood", wherein hollow cheeks so-called super stars are getting paid through the nose the main chunk of the production cost in the name of nepotism for their wooden actions.

The casting couch syndrome is the demanding of sexual favours by an employer or person in a position of power and authority, from an apprentice employee, or sub ordinate to a superior in return for entry into an occupation, or for other career advancement within an organization.

The term casting couch originated in the motion picture industry, with specific reference to couching in offices that could be used for sexual activity between casing directors or film producers and aspiring actors.

Within the adult entertainment industry, content featuring fictitious casting couch scenarios has become a popular niche.

Notable Casting Couch Remarks and Incidents:

United States

The legend of the Hollywood casting couch coincided with the rise of the studio system in the 1910s.Several mogul producers were rumored to have enthusiastic practitioners, and it has been claimed that many actresses attempted, with varying degrees of success, to attain stardom via this route.

In 1945, Maureen O'Hara was quoted as saying, "I don't let the producer and director kiss me every morning or let them paw me. In 2004, she repeated: "I wouldn't throw myself on the casting couch, and I know that cost me parts.

In a 1966 interview, actor Woody Harrelson declared "every [acting] business I ever entered into in New York seemed to have a casting couch...I've seen so many people sleep with people they loath in order to further their ambition.

At a 2005 class reunion, producer Chris Hanley told his former classmates that "almost every leading actress in all of [his] 24 films have slept with a director or producer or a leading actor to get the part that launched her career.

In 2017, Lance Bass of 'N Sync wrote that "as a society, we've been become far too comfortable with the pervasive 'casting couch' adage that it no longer resembles what it truly is-sexual assault. ... I grew up in the entertainment business and I've experienced my share of unwanted advances from both men and women who saw me a target.

In July 2016, television executive Roger Ailes was accused of sexual harassment by former Fox News Channel anchor Gretchen Carlson. More than twenty other women, including Megyn Kelly and Andrea Tantaros, have since come forward with similar allegations about Ailes predatory casting couch-like behavior in the television industry over 50-year period. Since then, Fox's Bill O'Reilly has also been accused by multiple women of sexual harassment; $45 million has so far been paid to six women.

On 1 November 2016, defense lawyers for Bill Cosby, who has been accused of sexual assault by over 60 women, wrote that, "Even if proven (and it could not be), the age-old 'casting couch' is not unique to Mr.Cosby, and thus not a 'signature' nor a basis for the admissibility of these witnesses' stories, let alone a conviction. (Cosby was convicted of sexual assault charges on April 26th, 2018)

On 25 May 2018, Harvey Weinstein's attorney Benjamin Brafman imparted that Weinstein "did not invent the casting couch in Hollywood." Brafman also later stated: "My job is to defend specific allegations of sexual misconduct, not the issue of the Hollywood casting couch over the last 30 or 100 years," before apologizing for using the term "casting couch" and saying that he would "never "use the phrase again.

Europe

In 1956, British fan magazine *Picturegoer* published a four-part casting–couch expose entitled "The perils of Show Business" featuring interviews with actresses such as Joy Webster, Dorinda Stevens, Anne Heywood and Marigold Russell.

In 2002, actress Lesley-Anne Down spoke of finding fame in the late 1960s: "The casting couch was full swing, people expected it... My teen-age years were pretty intense, a lot of pressure and a lot of horrible old men out there. In a 1977 interview, she had also said: "I was promised lots of lovely big films parts by American producers if I went to bed with them... Believe me, the casting couch is no myth."

In 2013, Myleene Klasss stated that, "I don't think there's a single person in the entertainment industry that hasn't, at some point, experienced the casting couch thing." Earlier, in 2010, she revealed a major Hollywood star (named in 2017 as Harvey Weinstein) wanted to sign a sex contract with her.

Asia

In 2003 and 2006, Chinese actress Zhang Hao(张钰) released several graphic audio recordings and sex videos that she made herself to document her allegations that she won roles through the casting couch. The videos were released on You Tube but have been subsequently removed.

In 2011, India TV unveiled a series of exposes on the Bollywood casting couch using hidden cameras. They showed young actresses routinely being asked by male personalities including actors, directors and producers to sleep with them in return for favors such as good word to another director or producer. In a follow up interview by BBC, Shakti Kapoor described "Will you co-operate with me" as the code that was used by the Bollywood industry as a proposal to sleep with that person in return for a film role. Other Bollywood entities corroborated this.

In March 2017, South Indian actress Varalaxmi Sarathkumar tweeted about being propositioned by the programming head of leading TV channel and wrote that "I didn't come to the industry to be treated like a piece of meat." Other Tollywood actresses have made similar accusation.

In April 2018, Sri Reddy, an Indian film actress, stripped herself in the public and protested against sexual harassment in the film industry.

Tailpiece

The casting couch culture is existing in the silver screen all over the world. It is not unusual since acting is after all an emotional blackmailing and those who love, live and breathe movies 24/7, what can more be expected out of their reel lives except this. One workplace wherein this kind of menace or evil of sexual exploitation can't find room is hard-headed real-life people live in.

CHAPTER FOUR

IS CORONA CHINA MADE?

Is nature settling its score through Corona virus? Don't know, only time will tell! The world had battled out SARS, MERS, EBOLA and NIPAH before. Now together wagering war against the Corona virus globally. Certainly, world would overcome this quagmire situations once.

The Novel Coronavirus of 2019 or Nco V-2019, which proved that small is not beautiful anymore as it appears and at the same time distrustful and horrific also!? The reason for this observation is as simple as people-to-people connections have become unapproachable and unseen and it has put people in quarantine and in isolation for a period of forty days minimum or double of it or more for maximum.

The worst part of the situation is lockdown, whether it may be imposed by either any of the state governments or the central government, which eventuate in curtailment of locomotion of its citizens. People who do not stay at home at this point of time, may be either homeless or one who may be out of his stock or out of his senses.

The most afflicted people are going to be the rural poor and the urban poor respectively in this trying time. They are punished for no faults of theirs indeed, rather the faults of the urban rich and educated and the rural rich and educated. The principle of "no work no pay" would be squarely applied to a daily wager who seldom own a passport and therefore does not travel abroad usually. As far as the poor are concerned, these are the lean days ahead and they are left in the lurch!

The medium, either print or digital, are come under the purview of ESMA, the Essential Services Maintenance Act, 1968, (which is a law made by the Parliament of India under List No.33 in Concurrent List of 7th Schedule of Constitution of India), hence these main means of the mass communication maintain national uniformity by spreading genuine and reliable news of the coronavirus across the country by day and night. Though lockdown is making the newspaper bundles lean of everyone who are becoming fat day by day by voracious eating in this stay-at-home period.

This is a phase wherein White Army (Doctors and all other hospital staff) are fighting in the frontline against the Covid-19 making hospitals as battle grounds, while the Khaki Army (Police) are on the roads literally all these passing days patrolling and route marching in every nook and cranny of the streets searching for the errant travelers.

Lockdown period is case down period too! If there aren't cases occurred in the nature of road accidents like hit-and run, drunken driving, and cases included in the categories of theft, theft in dwelling house, lurking house–trespass by night, and cases of highly talkable and deceitful in nature like bank robbery and dacoity, etc. And now everybody is practicing social distancing and even one of the richest lawyers in the world is not an exception in these testing times like Michelle Obama (Ex.First Lady of U.S.A).

The Ministry of Finance (India) and as well as the Reserve Bank of India (RBI) have announced so many sops by way of economic packages and moratoriums amid the coronavirus outbreak and resultant national lockdown in the country and one or two of them is/are to provide relief to around 14 Lakhs taxpayers, besides all pending GST and custom refunds would be released benefiting close to 1 Lakh businessmen. Of course, tax payers are included both salaried people and un-salaried people. The International Labor Organization (ILO) estimates that only 22% of India's workforce falls under the category of salaried employment while 78% had no assured salary. So, how many people (percentage) will be included in the 14 Lakhs taxpayers out of the 78 percentage (%) people?

Suppose, if I am a salaried employee, I should pay salary to my cook or maid if he or she works on salary basis, he or she does not loss his or her salary in this scenario, if he or she is a salaried employee, since government has strictly warned that any kind of salary cut is not allowed in this lockdown period by the employer. If I get salary in this off-working days simply staying at home, I have to pay the same to him or her who is as well staying at his or her home in this lockdown period. This "give and take" policy proposed by the government is good in this juncture. My hair cut is due for weeks now due to the lockdown. Then what about barbers, carpenters and masons,etc. From these skilled laborer's how many are included and how many are excluded in the above said math's of 22% and 78%. They answer shall be that the majority are distanced from the former and belonged to the latter who may be considered as the major labor force in a country like India.

This out of the blue lockdown period is going to be beneficial to those women whose husbands are in the bad habits of smoking or drinking. They can breathe of fresh air in their husbands' behavior now. And definitely several fathers and mothers will get back their teenaged or adult sons and daughters from these life style bad habits, and of all, the most beneficent group would be mother and son.

Film industry is one of the entertainment fields, which has been worse hit by this pandemic lockdown world over. This is an occasion to learn new skills on internet. I am personally practicing new scales and caged methods on guitar now. The budding artists are more affected than established ones and they are primary casualties in each and every field of it.

This is a period wherein domestic violence cases are bulking out day by day as per the data released by the NCW

(The National Commission for Women). It is an irony that in this home quarantine/isolation period, quarrels and harassments are taken place randomly in this sweet stay at home period on account of country-wide lockdown imposed to control the spread of coronavirus. What is the cause? Is this that men are not used to stay at home full time? Would frustration and stress change a person's temperament? The women are strong enough in fighting off the novel coronavirus than men, but it seems strange that they are defenseless before the harassments, which their husbands (less viruses) are indulged in for time pass in this stay-at-home period of complete national lockdown.

The President has spoken to the nation about the covid-19, which pandemic has led to many countries announcing a lockdown and the Prime Minister who has locked the nation down before two weeks ago in his announcement to the nation.

In this context, let us take "go corona, corona go" slogan in a lighter vein instead of labelling its coined minister as a covidiot! The question is where to go this World Wide Web coronavirus. Where else except www.com, i. e. internet itself?! If the intent and goal of the coronavirus is mass destruction, please go away corona and infect internet and thereby deleting one and all fallacious, illegitimate, illegal and malicious contents in the forms of applications, files, programs and sites in the virtual world!

We can hope that there is light at the end of the tunnel because coronavirus comes from China, and China product lacks guarantee and warranty, and therefore its reliability and durability are at stake! The coronavirus is also a made in China product, whether it is created or generated, in either case, it is perishable sooner or later. It is controversial that although made in China has a good (or bad) intention of being products making from China, critics of China have utilized to mock low products or misbehaviors as "Made in China" in order to criticize the Chinese Government for its mishandling, censorship, propaganda, imperialism and public misbehaviors. I could infer a new mantra from this stay at home in the time of coronavirus-cum-lockdown period is that what I just want to amend "health is wealth" (Old) as "wisdom is wealth" (New)?!

AppendiX: I support lockdown and eagerly waiting for more tasks coming from the PM.

CHAPTER FIVE

MODI OPERANDI

Minimum Government, Maximum Governance

Whether the promise of maximum governance, at the same time limiting the number of government portfolios, has been achieved by the impending government at the Centre. Are Minimum government for make in India, digital India, startup India and standup India all means to an end of attaining maximum governance!?

Make in India

Make in India was launched on 25 September 2014 covering more than 25 sectors of the economy, such as Automobiles, Automobile components, Aviation, Biotechnology, Chemicals, Construction, Defense manufacturing, Defense exports, Electronic systems, Electrical machinery, Food processing, Exports, Information technology and business process management, Leather, Media and entertainment, Mining, Oil and gas, Pharmaceuticals, Ports and shipping, Railways, Renewable energy, Roads and highways, Space and astronomy, Thermal power, Textiles and garments, Tourism and hospitality, and Wellness and Healthcare.

To cover for the make in India initiative, government introduced the digital India campaign and its monstrous evils affected the common people in the forms of demonetization and GST subsequently.

Digital India

Digital India is a campaign to ensure the government's services are made available to citizens electronically by improved online infrastructure and by increasing internet connectivity or by making the country digitally empowered in the field of technology. In brief, to connect rural India with the digital India! Launched on 1 July 2015.

The Indian population is broadly divided into two, rural and urban. The rural population is two times the urban population of India. Agriculture and farming are still main sources of income of the rural population and they are transacting in terms of real money only. A full-fledged agribusiness is yet to attain momentum in rural India.

If anybody scratches one's head and asks whether the skill India, which was launched on 15 July 2015 aims to train over 40 crore people in India in different skills by 2022, is the by-product of the make in India and the digital India, can we give a convincing answer to it. Or, the make in India and the digital India have been derived from the skill India!

Startup India

A startup defined as an entity that is headquartered in India, which was opened less than seven years ago, and has an annual turnover less than 25 crore. The action plan of this initiative is based on the following three pillars: simplification and hand-holding, funding support and incentives and industry-academia partnership and incubation. The event was inaugurated on 16 January 2016.

As far as India and its circumstances are concerned, politics is investment free and more profitable business.

Stand up India

Launched the stand-up India scheme on 5 April 2016 as part of the government's efforts to support entrepreneurship among women and SC & ST communities. Definitely, if the UPA-3 is coming to power in the upcoming Lok Sabha elections, they are going to retain this scheme at least in its letter and spirit.

The proposed prime ministerial candidate of the congress party has chosen Wayanad in Kerala as his second constituency. The density of tribal population is decent there. So, visiting tribal huts and dine and stay with them shall be any more a problem for the potential premier since now.

Rahul Vs Modi=Rafale!

The saga of rafale had begun from 31 January 2012 and continued over the period of all these years and ended temporarily on 14 December 2018 in the Supreme Court. The scapegoat was the Hindustan Aeronautics Limited (HAL) between the fight by the National Democratic Alliance and the United Progressive Alliance.

It is understandable that Mr.Mukesh Ambani helping his younger brother Mr.Anil Ambani to clear the latter dues in terms of money. But it is undigested that the lone wolf prime minister supporting his industrialist friend in getting an offset contract for his private defense company by sidelining the defense public sector undertaking HAL from the French company Dassault Aviation. During an official visit to France in April 2015, prime minister announced that India would acquire 36 fully built rafale citing critical operational necessity. In July 2015, defense minister informed the Rajya Sabha that the tender for 126 aircraft had been withdrawn and negotiations for 36 aircraft had begun!

Consequently, in September 2016, after clearance from the Indian Cabinet Committee on Security, India and France signed an inter-governmental agreement (IGA) for the acquisition of 36 aircraft. The agreement included a 50% offset clause, which required the companies involved in the agreement to invest 50% of the contract value back into India. On 3 October 2016, Reliance Group and Dassault Aviation issued a joint statement announcing the creation of a 51:49 joint venture named Dassault Reliance Aerospace Limited (DRAL), to focus on aero structures, electronics and engine components as well as to foster research and development projects under the Indigenously Designed Developed and Manufactured (IDDM) initiative.

Wolf in Sheep's Clothing

Instead of keeping the wolf from the doors of thousands of Indians, the incumbent central government had compromised on the national security by inducting a private defense company in the place of a state-owned HAL.Is it national interest or personal interest? Is it make in India or make in corporate? Indian prime minister should not be steep like Lalit Modi, Nirav Modi, etc. in case of defense dealings at the cost of national security.

The rough must be taken with the smooth. The thing is that whether you want a strong prime minister or a gentle prime minister who bill and coo and consciously not indulging in double speaking in public.

Whether the potential prime ministerial candidate of the congress party has the ability to pull in horns of the current pm. Before writing or laughing off the prospective gentle man prime ministerial nominee of the congress party, looks at what he and his party did in both houses of parliament and outside to book the present Modi's government in rafale deal. The persistence by Rahul in case of rafale itself showed that he has become a filtered seasoned politician over the period of time. He pursued the rafale case single handily which proved his leadership quality. India's more than 50% of its population below the age of 25 and more than 65% below the age of 35 will not go unseen it. Genuine fear of unemployment. Rahul Gandhi and Priyanka Gandhi are no longer like back wheels of a car. They have grown out of their apprenticeship of politics.

Though the culture of the congress party is not a pleased one, but okay comparing to other political parties narrowcast approach such as the Left and BJP who are followed the same suit in the matter of elections of its politburo that of hierarchical caste politics. When will a SC/ST comrade be there in the politburo of Indian communist parties before losing national party status to the said parties?

Forecast

The coming Lok Sabha elections will be mainly versus Rural Vs Urban, Unemployed Vs Employed, Individual Vs Corporate, Woman Vs Man, Unorganized Vs Organized, Young Vs Old, and Agricultural Vs Nonagricultural. Are all these enough to satisfy the above issues in terms of healthcare for the poor, ten percent reservation for economically weaker sections, cash support to farmers apart from Bharat Net, Industrial Corridors, Bharatmala, Sagarmala, Dedicated Freight Corridors and Udan-Rcs and E-Krantic. Besides, e-sampark, Insolvency and Bankruptcy code, Goods and Services tax, direct benefit transfers,

Swachh Bharat, Jan Dhan Yojana and Aadhaar.

Achhe Din and Swachh Bharat

It was a dream come true when we heard first time about good days were coming way back in 2014 Lok Sabha election! But, were the ways and means of the elected central government up to the mark thinking in a common man or farmer point of view. It was all paper tiger will be the answer. Swachh Bharat Mission should aim too to clean up Politian, bureaucrat, nepotist and whoever it may be who were corrupted by power, then only Achhe Din will come!

A corrupt bureaucracy is a curse and the main culprit in a nation's development and progress. Bureaucracy is a minority group like elected representatives in the vast majority population of a country. The majority is always governed or ruled by these minorities of the officials or the elected representatives. An elected representative or a leader should not necessarily be a good ruler, but what makes an elected representative a leader or a ruler of his or her party's mandate in the election. A ruler is a back-seat driver and the front-seat driver shall be a bureaucrat or advisor who would be in every inch in an incompetent leader's ruling.

This writer does not vouch for any particular political party here, but whatever or whoever it may be, promises are to be kept, unfulfilled promises would be like Sangalp or Maya, and that will boomerang!

CHAPTER SIX

MOLESTATION vs. DEMONETIZATION:

If the Demonetization drive (8/11/2016) was an attack against the black money and its allied menaces, the New Year's Eve Mass Molestation at central business district in Bengaluru and following incidents in other parts of the city were an attack on women irrespective of all age groups, young, middle and old.

A woman approached police, saying an unidentified man pulled her T-shirt. The incident occurred at 9.p.m, when the victim was returning home from the gym. Is there anything to do with the incident of that of the said demonetization drive here? Are these attacks on women in Bengaluru and across every city in our country a reverse repercussion of the said demonetization exercises?

One cannot furnish substantial evidence linking the untoward incidents to the demonetization, but if you are asking whether the stress and anger it caused attributed to such happenings massively in Bengaluru and other parts of the country after the demonetization, the answer is not a blatant No(t)! But such incidents have been occurring for centuries, which we cannot deny.

The death of one Kallol Roychowdhury on December 4, at around 7.30.p.m was one among over 80 people, who died awaiting their turn to withdraw money suffered from heart ailments, hypertension, diabetes and other age-related ailments.

One of the incidents of NYE molestation in Bengaluru is that where miscreants were trying to sexually abuse a woman at midnight. A woman was walking alone on the road side at around 2.40 a.m, when two two-wheeler-borne miscreants stopped next to her. One of the riders got down from the vehicle, groped (reminds of Mr.Trump) the girl and started kissing (again) her and dragged her to his friend (for him to molest her too) sitting on the two-wheeler.

The woman tried to fight with the pervert, but he then hugged her and pulled her towards his associate who was sitting on the two-wheeler.

The due molested her and tried to pull her on to the two-wheeler to ride away, but she screamed loudly for help, after which the miscreants speed away, pushing her onto the road.

"Youngsters are almost like Westerners...not only in mindset but even in their dressing" What does it mean? Is that girls and boys are clothed in minis and Bermuda respectively?!Is it due to the demonetization that has given severe hardship to the youth to make their ends meet in cladding!

The people are in stress and tenseness nowadays, especially the youth in lower income strata. In case of Kammanahalli (Bengaluru), Sadashivanagar, Diary Circle molestation-to name just a few, the molesters are all youth (average to 22 years) and comparatively less earners like delivery(food) boys, Manson and driver, etc.

I haven't heard any such untoward incident of mass molestation on the eve of the New Year celebration in Bengaluru over the last one decade. The girls who gather there in every year in their modern outfit as usual and they do smoke and drink as their boys' counterparts do.

Dear ladies you have got equality before law or the equal protection of the laws within the man-made laws, women have equal rights, respect and protection and after all women are equal to men as per the said laws, but certainly not by *lex-aeterna*. The nightmarish mayhem of the said molestation on the occasion of the New Year's Eve celebration in Bengaluru has proved it right, not by one way but many!

I have no comments on western dressing, our forefathers were not different from it, but in respect of mindset, I have strong objection. What I am driving at is mindlessness than a mere mindset.

"On New Year or X-mas Day...these kinds of things happen...Youngsters are almost like Westerners. Not only in mindset but even in their dressing. So, some disturbance, some girls are harassed, these kinds of things do happen."

If the minister's statement has not been misconstrued, it would be like "Youngsters are almost like Westerners...they are mindless and therefore poor in dressing. So, some disturbance, some girls are harassed, these kinds of things do happen."

According to law of nature, man and woman are not created physically, mentally and emotionally as the same. A man cannot be a woman in its true sense, similarly a woman ought not to try to become a man.

Even the westerners (ladies) lack hair on their upper lips, yet they do party, sing, dance and get together with their male counterparts to welcome the New Year at Times square in every year.

Despite of 1,500 police officers present at Bengaluru's CBD, the women in a crowd-wherein majority of people were drunk-welcoming 2017, were molested.

The real reason behind the mass molestation is majority of Indian men who think women are at their disposal, that they can have authority over a woman, that if she is drunk, she is inviting.

Is this the real reason behind the Bengaluru Mass molestation on New Year's Eve, as reported by some viral news? The answer is also a blatant Not. Are all Indian men mindful to do so in public, when they are out of their senses? No-nonsense!?

CHAPTER SEVEN

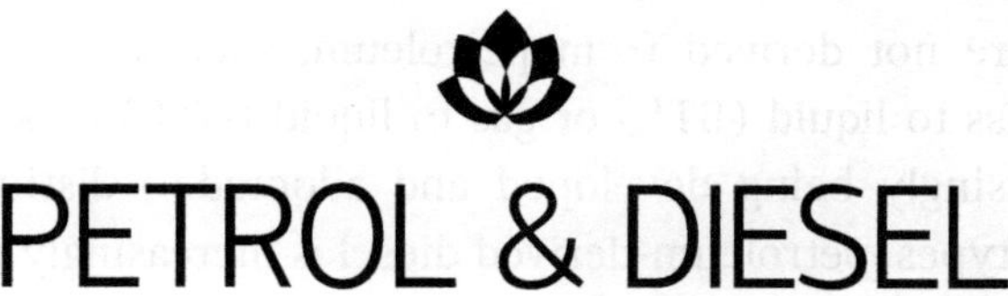

PETROL & DIESEL

Petrol and diesel are nearing to the categories of those precious metal like platinum and nonmetal like diamond in terms of its price, in point of time, are concerned. People are scared to spell petrol and diesel nowadays so that it shall be meaningful as well as appropriate to name the former as one Mr.Mucash and another Mr.Pradan respectively.

Petrol, a fluid consisting of a mixture of refined petroleum hydrocarbons, primarily consisting of octane, commonly used as a motor fuel. Diesel, in general is any liquid fuel used in diesel engines, whose fuel ignition takes place, without any spark, as a result of compression of the inlet air mixture and then injection of fuel.

The most common type of diesel fuel is a specific fractional distillate of petroleum fuel oil, but alternatives that are not derived from petroleum, such as biodiesel, biomass to liquid (BTL) or gas to liquid (GTL) diesel, are increasingly being developed and adopted.to distinguish these types, petroleum-derived diesel is increasingly called Petro diesel.

Natural Resources

Natural resources are resources that exist without actions of humankind. This includes all valued characteristics such as magnetic, gravitational, electrical properties and forces etc. Natural resources may be further classified in different ways. Natural resources are materials and components (something that can be used) that can be found within the environment. Every man-made product is composed of natural resources (at its fundamental level). A natural resource may exist as a separate entity such as fresh water, air and as well as a living organism such as a fish, or it may exist in an alternate form that must be processed to obtain the resource such as metal ores, rare earth metals, petroleum, and most forms of energy.

Types of Natural Resources

Biotic-Biotic resources are obtained from the biosphere (living and organic material), such as forest and animals, and the material that can be obtained from them.

Fossil Fuels-such as coal and petroleum are also included in this category because they are formed from decayed organic matter.

Potential Resources

Potential resources are those that may be used in the future, and petroleum being a potential resource, like government see some corporate, which in sedimentary rocks that, until drilled out and put to use remains a potential resource. When the government is going to realize that those so called stalwart corporate entities are like non-renewable resources, once they are indebted, either they leave the country or the government takes years to get it repaid. So, corporate sector in India is not renewable resources as far as our prior experiences are concerned, which is still continuing to be a non-renewable resource of private sector.

Neck and Neck

Until an effective checks and balances system for government in the policies and programs of petroleum sector emerged, with global crude oil price fluctuation, the period of high oil prices is now over all over the world, but in our country, it is still skyrocketing crossing all the boundaries. Petrol and diesel prices are appearing to be competing to each other for reaching towards century point and by the time this piece of writing is getting published, it might happen. Anyhow, unless government mends its policy to rob Peter to pay Paul, nothing is going to be changed.

Rules are to be changed

Whether the changes are vertical or horizontal, it doesn't matter, but, ultimately, the beneficiaries should be the common people who make ends meet. The Provisions of the Petroleum Act,1934(30 Of 1934), or the rules made there under, are the legal tools of government to consolidate and amend the law relating to the import, transport, storage, production, refining and blending of petroleum.

The Petroleum and Natural Gas Rules deals with the Petroleum exploration license & Petroleum Mining Lease, and the Petroleum and Natural Gas Regulatory Board constituted under the Petroleum and Natural Gas Regulatory Board Act, to protect the interests of consumers and entities engaged in specified activities relating to petroleum, petroleum products and natural gas and promote competitive markets and for matters connected therewith or incidental thereto.

Petrol and diesel are up to common men neck and at this juncture it seems that the government can only do one thing to alleviate the poor that is nothing but to allow the oil companies to price petroleum products at rates more than their import price and reducing the market rates instead of increasing it on daily basis as rightly does by the government as a routine on petroleum and diesel rates, thereby government can eyewash the poor for time being.

In other way, the prices of petroleum and diesel are to be adjusted in agreement with the import parity price, this way the government can reduce the price of petroleum and diesel by pittance, say 2.50 rupees, after increasing it ten times more on the daily basis.

It is estimated that the world consumes about 95 million barrels each day. Consumption is currently around 84 million barrels (13.4×10^6 m^3) per day, or 4.9 km^3 per year, yielding a remaining oil supply of only about 120 years, if current demand remains static.

Alternatives to Petroleum –Based Vehicle Fuels

Today, about 90 percent of vehicular fuel needs are met by oil. Vehicles that use alternative fuels used in standard or modified internal combustion engines such as natural gas vehicles, neat ethanol vehicles, flexible-fuel vehicles, biodiesel-powered vehicles, propane auto gas, and hydrogen vehicles. There is much debate worldwide over natural resource allocations; this is particularly true during periods of increasing scarcity and shortage (depletion and over consumption of resources) but also because the exploration of natural resources is the basis.

Bullock Cart Governance Vs. Petroleum Governance

A time where petrol and diesel be manufactured like drugs or chemicals in a laboratory and for the commodity it shall be anything other than the crude oil like leaves, water or even air, then only, it seems that the petrol and diesel prices are going to be less or cheap. Otherwise, people are to get ready to experience with bullock cart by shedding their egos to commute to and fro, width and breadth, vertical and horizontal and up and down. Is it bullshit? Any government, centralor states, which pave the way for its people to go back to ancient times, wherein bullock cart or ox cart were there, is a progressive government. Nope. Bullock cart or ox cart were not the things of past, they are still used today where modern vehicles are too expensive or the infrastructures favor them. Yup. It was a means of transportation and as well as for goods used in many parts of the world.

CHAPTER EIGHT

"PIL FOR EVERY ILL"

This is the era of PILs. A PIL (Public Interest Litigation) is the modern legal first aid to the sickening society for various reasons. It acts as a medicine pill which treats or prevents diseases in human body likewise each PIL is a drug to cure the illnesses of the societies caused by various lawlessness. Nowadays advocate is not merely a court officer but he has become a society doctor also. When a family doctor administers medicine to an ailing patient, an advocate files PIL petition for social welfare as a whole.

If Hippocrates was the father of medicine, Justice P.N.Bhagwati was the man behind the idea of PIL in India. The framers of Indian constitution did not incorporate a strict doctrine of separation of powers but envisaged a system of checks and balances. Policy making and implementation of policy are conventionally regarding as the exclusive domain of the executive and the legislature. The PIL has a great role to play in equalizing the activities of the three organs of the government, viz; legislature, executive and judiciary.

The Public Interest Litigation emerged in S.P.Gupta and Others Vs. President of India and Others, (AIR 1982 SUPREME COURT 149). A PIL can be filed on various matters touching the society in general and important issues must be flagged in each PIL, larger public issues, such as human rights, consumer welfare and environmental, etc.

Here are some of the famous Public Interest Litigation cases which have changed our society tremendously. Sheela Barse Vs.State of Maharashtra, Sheela Barse's PIL (AIR 1983 SC 378). It was one of the many milestones of the PILs that dealt with the issue of custodial violence against women. That was for separate lock-ups for women convicts from their male counterparts. It was a land mark judgment by which separate police lock-ups for women convicts were allowed in Indian prisons. The next famous PIL was M.C.Mehta Vs. Union of India (Pollution in the Ganga) (AIR 1997 SUPREME COURT 378) filed on the basis of environmental issues. It was the beginning of green litigation in India.

When the court kept its distance from policy decisions was challenged by the Supreme Court in 2001.The disinvestment season initiated by the government to sell 51% stake in BALCO (Bharat Aluminium Company Limited). The Supreme Court in its decision said that PIL is not a pill or a panacea for all wrongs.

A PIL is an extraordinary remedy available at a cheaper cost to all citizens of the country who are denied basic human rights to whom freedom and liberty have no meaning otherwise. It ought not to be used by all litigants as a substitute for ordinary ones or as a means to file frivolous complaints. The advocates have to mention new issues and grievances affecting the society in common before the courts from time to time to provide valuable judgments from the courts. One may not get profited from the judgment individually, but which will be directly or indirectly benefited to one-by-one way or other without any demur.

The judiciary has chosen not to encroach on the authority of the government and its policy decisions. The judges have also drawn a line distinguishing between the domain of the executive and the judiciary in a bid to avoid the clash between the two. Thus, the PIL judgment read that the Public Interest Litigation was not meant to be a weapon to challenge the financial or economic decisions which are taken by the government in exercise of their administrative powers. But the Supreme Court subsequently chose to step into and criticized the policy decision first-come-first-served as the basis to allocate natural resources. The court's advice was to use auctions for all allocations. Even though some saw it through the prism of judicial overreach that did not stop the top court from scrapping of 122 2G licenses.

The Public Interest Litigation means litigation for safeguard of interest of public in general. It is a system of ligation in a court of law, not by the aggrieved party but by the court itself or by any other private party, for a general cause or grievance. It is not necessary that the person who is the victim of the violation of his or her right shall personally approach the court. Usually, advocates are the mediums between the petitioner and the court. But the litigant filing the petition shall prove before the court that the petition being filed for a public interest than that of a personal grievance.

The Public Interest Litigation has to go a long way and let it have a good future considering the people from diverse backgrounds in India. The traditional rule of right of a party to appear and be heard before a court has been considerably relaxed by the Supreme Court in its recent decisions. Now, the courts permit Public Interest Litigation for the enforcement of constitutional or legal rights. Any public welfare minded citizen can approach the court for the general cause in the interests of the public by filing a PIL petition in Supreme Court under Art.32 of the Constitution or in High Court under Art.226 of the Constitution.

Justice V.R.Krishna lyer in Fertilizer Corporation Kamagar Union (Regd.) Sindri and Others Vs. Union of India and Others, (AIR 1981 SUPREME COURT 344) enumerated the following reasons for liberalization of the rule of locus standi that the exercise of state power to eradicate corruption may result in unrelated interference with individuals' rights. Social justice warrants liberal judicial review administrative action. Restrictive rules of standing are antithesis to a liberal system of administrative action. So, activism is essential for participative public justice. Therefore, a public minded citizen must be given an opportunity to move the court in the interests of the public.

Public Interest Litigation is the power given to the public by the courts through its judicial activism. That a person, whose right is infringed alone, can file a petition, is the gone are the days now. Three have been in recent times increasingly instances of abuse of PILs. Such cases may occur when the victim does not have the necessary resources to commence litigation or his freedom to move court has been suppressed or encroached upon. The court can itself take cognizance of the matter and precede suo motu or cases can commence on the petition of any public-spirited individual. Therefore, there is a need to re-emphasize the parameters within which PIL can be resorted to by a petitioner and entertained by the court. Sometimes the Courts are in a fix that the PIL(s) may be like a bittersweet pill at times that the Judge(s) can neither spit nor swallow it because of its dual taste. Anyhow, in either case, in the interest of general public, long live for PILs.

CHAPTER NINE

VERIFICATION OF PROPERTY DOCUMENTS

It is very necessary to verify property documents before going to purchase any immovable property anywhere in India including Bengaluru. Both the title deeds and the subsidiary documents in respect of the title of each and every immovable property are to be verified by an expert in this regard before entering into any contractual agreements or obligations to ascertain whether the property intended to buy is good or free from all kinds of encumbrances, such as, minor claims, litigation, and maintenance, to name just a few.

Title Deeds:

The title deed or deeds, whichever term is referred to name it, it is the most important and main document by which possession or ownership of a property has been changed from one person to another or others.it shall not always be a sale deed but anything though which property transaction has to be made, for e.g., lease deed, mortgage deed, gift deed, or release deed, etc.

The title deed is like a foundation of a building and if the foundation is not strong enough to stand up on its own base, further construction of any number of floors built up on it will be in a risk at any time in future. We can see one title deed or a few numbers of title documents for an immovable property, but it is pertinent to take note that even though there are several numbers of title documents for an immovable property, there shall be only one title deed for a property at a point in time and the rest of other title document or documents shall be in series to a present one which is counted as the original title deed of an immovable property.

The title deed shall not always be one in number, but there may have two or more at the same time for an immovable property depending on the kind of transactions by which change of ownership of a property had been taken place earlier amongst its erstwhile parties. But, remember one thing that, if the title deed or deeds are one or two or more, every title deed or deeds shall be current or and connected to each other in case the title deeds are more than one to a certain immovable property.

Series of Title Deeds:

If someone goes and scrutinizes the available title documents presented by a present owner of an immovable property, the history of derivation of title by the present owner can very well be ascertained from that series or chains of previous title documents brought out by the present owner pertaining to his immovable property. The number of past title documents vary from one immovable property to another and it is purely depended on as to how many times owners had changed hands of his or her property in the past from time to time over a period from one to another. These earlier title document or documents pertaining to an immovable property are known as mother deed/s or parent deed/s.in brief, it is the title document or documents just prior to the original title deed or deeds.

Tracing of Title Deeds:

There are four types of title, broadly, but for practical convenience, title can be divided into two types, original and derivative. The example for original title is title by succession and for derivative title is purchase.

Subsidiary Documents:

Verification of property documents, also includes verification of subsidiary documents relating to an immovable property. It is part and parcel of the whole process of analyzing, reviewing and also calls for any additional required documents from the concerned party for suiting a better title to a potential buyer to whom acquisition of property takes place once in a lifetime. A lawyer's duty is to safeguard the interest of his client.

A subsidiary property document can be anything except the present title deed or deeds of an immovable property, such as, tax paid receipt, mutation extract, khatha certificate, etc. When we say subsidiary property documents, it is mainly referred to the revenue documents of an immovable property.

In searching of the title of a property, these subsidiary documents are also played a pivotal role which may sometimes be a link connecting to one document to another in order to arrive at a correct conclusion of events of sequence and in chronological order.

Allied Documents:

As long as an immovable property of a site or a plot is laying vacant, it doesn't require a building sanctioned plan, commencement certificate, completion certificate, etc. But, the moment its owner plans to construct a house or an apartment complex on the very same site or plot, all these documents emerge and come into existence at once and as far as the said vacant site or plot is concerned those documents were once non-existent and irrelevant and without which the title of the said immovable property was good and perfect.

And, as far as an immovable property of a house or a flat is concerned, building license, plan sanction, occupancy certificate, etc., are very much important like the title and the subsidiary documents and all the above are come under the allied documents and in the absence of which title of a house property or an apartment complex shall not be perfect and valid.

The allied documents which were not relevant to an immovable property of a site or plot when the same was remained as vacant, but, get relevance once the said property's transformation from its earlier form (site or plot) into a new form (house or flat) and a allied document or documents which are widely ranged from panchayat's Khatha building license to airport authority's NOC (Height Clearance).

Conclusion:

A potential buyer will always be in search of a new and good property and after his or her month-long effort, if a property is identified as suitable and ideal, what shall be the next course of action be taken by as a first-time purchaser to proceed further in dealing with the property on a layman's point of view. Of course, to give advance, definitely, but, what type of advance. Token, advance amount or earnest money.

It is not advisable to give beyond a returnable token advance, which shall be refundable in the event of non-materialization of a deal due to any defect in title, by a buyer to a seller unless and until he or she gets a legal certificate/opinion from a competent expert in this respect. The sign of a legal opinion may not be always green to go further, but if the signal is red, wait until it turns green and proceed further by signing a sale agreement or contract after paying a substantial amount of consideration price as advance or earnest money to the seller, otherwise, you may be hassled from pillar to post to get back your hard-earned money from the seller or anybody representing through or under him or her through mediation or by well-wishers or in a court of law.

Last but not least that people are ready to give hundreds and thousands and lakhs of rupees in the name of bribe, but the very same people are not showing willingness to shell out a few thousands of rupees for their property documents verification which is considered as a reasonable cause and the first step in any kind of property investment. Buyers have no botheration about losing their money and they do pay scant attention to know their property appraisal report before venturing into any kind of property investment. What may come they will go ahead with their plan of buying a property merely on trust believing their agent, broker, middleman and finally seller as well without knowing whether the property they are going to own is good for their future investment and if at all it is a defective title property, they will be losing lakhs or crores of rupees for saving a few thousands of rupees as legal fees towards their due diligence of property documents verification.

CHAPTER TEN

YOUR LORDSHIP SHREE AYYAPPA SWAMY!

Man-made law is law that is made by humans, usually considered in opposition to concepts like natural or divine law. Man-made law was the lowest form of law, and man-made law ranked as fundamental because it is man-made. Its characteristics are that it is “not absolute”, and is created by human beings “above all “for the regulation of their actions and behavior (but also for the ordering of things). It “has to be generally known” and has to take into account [both] its anthropological determination and its chronological determination”. Man–made law is fluid, changing over time in order to adapt to changing real-world circumstances. In the Hegelian view, according to Professor Heinz Mohnhaupt.

According to Article 15 of the Constitution of India, 1950, the state shall not discriminate against any citizen on grounds only of religion, race, caste, sex, and place of birth or any of them. Yup.

No citizen shall, on grounds only of religion, race, caste, sex, and place of birth or any of them, be subject to any disability, liability, restriction or condition with regard to, what?

Access to shops, public restaurants, hotels and places of public entertainment or the use of wells, tanks, bathing ghats, roads and places of public resort maintained wholly or partly out of state funds or dedicated to the use of general public and including admission to educational institutions.

How far the above article shall be applicable to religious worship places? Pilgrim and tourist are not same and their entities are also entirely different. The former is governed by the natural rights and the latter is dealt with the legal rights.

Natural Rights and Legal Rights

Natural rights and legal rights are two types of rights. Natural rights are those that are not dependent on the laws or customs of any particular culture or government, and so are universal and inalienable (they cannot be repealed or restrained by human laws). Legal rights are those bestowed onto a person by a given legal system (they can be modified, repealed, and restrained by human laws.

The distinction between alienable and unalienable rights was introduced by Francis Hutcheson. In his *Inquiry into the Original of Our Ideas of Beauty and Virtue* (1725), Hutcheson foreshadowed the Declaration of Independence, stating: "For wherever any Invasion is made upon unalienable rights, there must arise either a perfect, or external Right to Resistance. Unalienable Rights are essential Limitations in all Government." Hutcheson elaborated on this idea of unalienable rights in his *A System of Moral Philosophy* (1755), based on the Reformation principle of the liberty of conscience. One could not in fact give up the capacity for private judgement (e.g., about religious questions) regardless of any external contracts or oaths to religious or secular authorities so that right is "unalienable." Hutcheson wrote: "Thus no man can really change his sentiments, judgements, and inward affection, at the pleasure of another; nor can it tend to any good to make him profess what is contrary to his heart. The right of private judgements is therefore unalienable.

Public Order and Social Order

According to Article 25 of the Constitution of India, 1950, all persons are equally entitled to freedom of conscience and the right freely to profess, practice and propagate religion, (1) Subject to public order, morality and health (i.e., social order) and to the other provisions of this Part, such as, (2) Nothing in this article shall affect the operation of any existing law or prevent the State from making any law-

(a) regulating or restricting any economic, financial, political or other secular activity which may be associated with religious practice;

(b) providing for social welfare and reform or the throwing open of Hindu religious institutions of a public character to all classes and sections of Hindus.

A straitjacket formula in religious ceremonies and practices are unconstitutional indeed, but at the same time applying a blanket rule on customs and traditions of religious affairs are also against the established social order and its contrast leads to public order crimes at large.

Therefore, certain reasonable restrictions on the part of courts can be imposed in the interest of public order, security of State, decency or morality and above all social order are concerned, since man and woman are not equal in the eyes of law of nature. Of course, equality before the law or the equal protection of the laws shall not deny to any person under the Constitution of India, 1950, because it is fundamental. But, at the same time, courts are to be more vigilant for public disorder and social disorder which may happen in the wake of judicial activism on sentimental matters, particularly on religious affairs. Otherwise, judiciary is dwarfed by legislature or executive.

Customs and Traditions

Custom is an established practice having the force of a law. Tradition, on the other hand, is something, such as a doctrine, belief, custom, story, etc., that is passed on from generation to generation, especially orally or by example. A custom (also called a tradition) is a common way of doing things. It is something that many people do, and have done for a long time. Usually, the people come from the same country, culture, or religion. Many customs are things that people do that are handed down from the past.

Though both are not same. The explanation of the meaning of custom and tradition looks similar. A custom can be a practice or belief that has been practiced an individual or a group for a long time. ... When a custom is transferred from generations to generation, it takes the form of tradition.

Suppose, if a High Court prohibited the entry of women above the age of 10 and below the age of 50(menstruating period) to a temple, but the Supreme Court overturned the ban on the entry of women, declaring that the selective ban on women was unconstitutional and discriminatory, who is right and who is wrong, whether the former is wrong or the latter is right?

Civil liberty is, in this respect, on the same footing with religious liberty. As no people can lawfully surrender their religious liberty by giving up their right of judging for themselves in religion, or by allowing any human beings to prescribe to them what faith they shall embrace, or what mode of worship they shall practice, so neither can any civil societies lawfully surrender their civil liberty by giving up to any extraneous jurisdiction their power of legislating for themselves and disposing their property. Wrote Price.

Menstruation and Nightfall

Menstruation and nightfall occur due to the rise and fall of hormones and hormone changes in a girl and in a boy respectively. The first menstrual circle usually begins between twelve and fifteen years of age in a girl, however, a period may occasionally start as young as eight years old and still be considered normal. Menstruation stops accruing after menopause, which usually occurs between

45 and 55 years of age in a woman. Menstruation and nightfall are body mechanism, which are controlled by biological clock.

Some women use hormonal contraception in this way to eliminate their periods for months or years at a time, a practice called menstrual suppression. Using synthetic hormones, it is possible for women to completely eliminate menstrual periods. When using progestogen implants, menstruation may be reduced to 3 or 4 menstrual periods per year. By taking progestogen-only contraceptive pills continuously without a 7-day span of using placebo pills, menstruation periods do not occur. Some women do this simply for convenience in the short-term while others prefer to eliminate altogether when possible.

Howsoever the argument seems watertight banning the entry of menstruating women from offering worship at Sabarimala shrine during any period of the year stating that such restriction was in accordance with the usage prevalent from time immemorial. Menstruation is a body clock. It can be eliminated in the shot-term or for a long term. So, what is the real riddle, menstruation or age?

Pilgrimage and Women

The devotees are expected to follow a 41-days austerity period prior to the pilgrimage. This begin with wearing of a special chain made of *Rudraksha* or *Tulas*i beads is commonly used. During the 41 days of austerity, the devotee who has taken the vow, is required to strictly follow the rules that include follow only a lacto-vegetarian diet, follow celibacy, follow teetotalism, not to use any profanity and have to control the anger, allow the hair and nails to grow without cutting. They must try their maximum to help others, and see everything around them as lord Ayyappa. They are expected to bath twice in a day and visit the local temples regularly and only wear plain black or blue colored traditional clothing.

Before the High Court 1991 verdict, women visited the Sabarimala temple even though in small numbers. Women pilgrims below the age of 50 would visit the temple to conduct the first rice-feeding ceremony of their children in the temple premises. The temple is situated on a hilltop amidst eighteen hills at an altitude of 480m (1,575 ft) above sea level, and surrounded by mountains and dense forests at the Periyar Tiger Reserve in Kerala, India. It is the largest annual pilgrimage in the world with an estimated 17-30 million devotees visiting every year. Some estimates put the number of annual visitors as high as 50 million. The temple is dedicated to the god Shri Ayyappan.

Hundreds of devotees still follow the traditional mountainous forest path (approximately 61 km), believed to be taken by Shri.Ayyappa himself. These days people use vehicles to reach the Pamba River by an alternate route. From Pamba, all the pilgrims begin trekking the steep mountain path of Neeli Mala till Sabari Mala. This route is now highly developed, with emergency shops and medical aid by the sides, and supporting aid is provided to the pilgrims while climbing the steep slope, which used to be mere trail through dense jungle. The elderly pilgrims are lifted by men on bamboo chairs till the top, on being paid.

As Martin Luther wrote: every man is responsible for his own faith, and he must see it for himself that he believes rightly. As little as another can go to hell or heaven for me, so little can he believe or disbelieve for me; and as little as he can open or shut heaven or hell for me, so little can he drive me to faith or unbelief. Since, then belief or unbelief is a matter of every one's conscience, and since this is no lessening of the secular power, the latter should be content and attend to its own affairs and permit men to believe one thing or another, as they are able and willing, and constrain no one force.

HC vs. SC

In 1991, justice K Paripoornan and justice K Balanarayana Marar of the Kerala High Court in their ruling against the Travancore Devaswom Board, banned entry of women between ages above 10 and below 50, from offering worship at Sabarimala Shrine, on the ground of usage prevalent from time immemorial, directing the Government of Kerala to use police force to implement and comply with the said order. But, on 28th September 2018 the Supreme Court, in a 4-1 majority decision, overturned the ban on women between the ages 10 and 50 entering the temple. Challenge was on the grounds of Article 15 & 25 of the Constitution of India, 1950, which are prohibition of discrimination on grounds of religion, race, caste, sex or place of birth and freedom of conscience and free profession, practice and propagation of religion respectively.

Whatever reasons put forth by the majority bench of the Supreme Court, while striking down the Kerala High Court 1991 ruling, which was constitutional so far as the special facts and circumstances of the Sabarimala Temple were concerned at that point in time.

9 798886 840223

Printed by Libri Plureos GmbH in Hamburg,
Germany